A SATURDAY NIGHT
AT THE FLYING DOG

And Other Poems

ALSO BY MARCIA SOUTHWICK

The Night Won't Save Anyone
Why the River Disappears

Limited editions:

What The Trees Go Into
Her Six Difficulties and His Small Mistakes
Connecticut: Eight Poems
Upon Hearing of a Drowning in the Connecticut River
Thaisa
The Leopard's Mouth Is Dry and Cold Inside, with Larry Levis

Anthology:

Extended Outlooks: The Iowa Review Collection of Contemporary Writing by Women, co-edited with Jane Cooper, Gwen Head and Adelaide Morris

A SATURDAY NIGHT AT THE FLYING DOG

And Other Poems

Marcia Southwick

Oberlin College Press

http://www.oberlin.edu/~ocpress

Library of Congress Cataloging-in-Publication Data

Southwick, Marcia
   A Saturday Night at the Flying Dog and other poems / Marcia Southwick.
      (The FIELD Poetry Series v. 8)
      I. Title.   II. Series.

LC: 99-60377
ISBN: 0-932440-85-1 (pbk.)

For Murray Gell-Mann, the "top quark"

TABLE OF CONTENTS

AUGURY

I've seen the future in a teacup, a pair of Nikes
and dust on a windowsill. I've seen it in a tire's skid marks,
on the blade of a barber's shears. All around me
two-income couples are buying title insurance.
They're scanning the stores for satellite dishes,
burglar alarms and new siding. They're playing tennis
at the country club with their trigger-happy teenagers.
And I want to tell them I've already seen the baby-boomers
die out. Everybody's checking out the Jerry Garcia
neckwear collection at Lord & Taylor and I want to tell them
God plays hardball. I'm already seeing flash floods,
and machine guns firing on the outskirts of town.
Rebels are slouching in buildings and emotions everywhere
are as volatile as Nasdaq. Waiting for us is a big splash,
a designer virus, nothing but automobile junkyards
and tattoo parlors. God's throwing a bash.
His storms send the crowds scurrying. Caddies
on golf courses strip down to their underwear
and pray in the rain, as God smiles with the immaculate
sheen of an airbrushed photo. After years of exile, he's
made his debut—a wizard of Oz with pectoral implants,
elevator shoes, and the face of one of the ten most wanted
deadbeat dads. And I want to say *stop!* Not everyone will own
a piece of the Martian meteorite. Not everyone will get
sexy abs in four weeks flat or be around to buy low-rise
boot-cut pants in polyester jersey. Not everyone will travel
the four-hundred-mile-long road through the jungles of Burma.
Not everyone's linden saplings, trained along chestnut branch-
trellises, will grow into a Gothic vault of greenery.

SMALL MIRACLES

Knitting lessons on the terrace. The old neighborhood
where every year the same woodchucks burrow down in the backyards.
Fireflies in a jar. You belong right here between the high pressure
over Alabama and gusty thunderstorms in Montana. Along with
Koko the Killer Clown and Illustrated Man who died in Chelsea,
covered with 35,000 tattoos. You don't need a new house with a tower-
view of the nightly fireworks at Epcot. You don't need
a purple merino wool long-sleeved turtleneck or its companion
charcoal & chalk-striped skirt in bi-stretch wool/nylon/spandex.
You just want to chase toddlers across the lawn instead of liberating
the entry hall from its dismally formal terrazzo floor
by replacing it with Italian limestone. It's a miracle. Your furniture
really does invigorate the rooms with nervy understatement.
You've been so busy investigating sexy new mutual funds
and watching Phyllis Diller, queen of the nip & tuck,
that you've totally forgotten to use less toxic household cleaner
and to practice natural lawn care by composting.
While sipping Bombay Sapphire martinis & listening
to the crooning voice of Julio Yglesias, you've forgotten
to cut back the raspberry canes and check for outbreaks
of white pine blister rust. You've forgotten your father
who hustled for tips carrying luggage at railroad station depots.
And *he'd* say: Skip the tuna tartare spiked with ponzu, chili oil and ginger.
Forget pears dropped into the poaching pot with little galaxies
of star anise. Back to cracked pepper and A-1 sauce.
But this is America, land of small miracles, where the Smirnoff
Fantasy Sweepstakes gets you to Cabo San Lucas,
and your highest goal is the perfectly struck golf ball.

TWENTY WAYS TO TIE A SARONG

I'm fleeing the city—back to pine trees
emerging from fog, and a bare-bones room in the old
woodland camp. I'll row across the Narrows to Hog Island,
frayed sheets, army blankets, and no maid service.
Want to come with me? We could whisper in the dark
about the guys. Or study sea slugs and try not to get fined
$500 for molesting a butterfly. Forget free-range chicken,
watercress salads, masseuses and wrap-around decks,
or bargains that include valet parking and Continental breakfast
for two. Let's canoe past pink dolphins on the Orinoco
instead of taking Celebrity Cruise's advanced Aqua Spa Program.
Let's go to Sabah & learn the twenty ways to tie a sarong
or look for puffins on East Egg Rock. Cough up the loot. We'll drive
the old Haul Road beyond the Arctic Circle all the way to Deadhorse.
And you're not to take so much as a single sea slug
from Hog Island. You're not to mention Sylvester Stallone.
You're not to fall for computer executives who can count
to 100 in Japanese. You can't listen to music by Mazzy Star,
the Cramps, Mystery Machine or the Rose Chronicles.
You're not to discuss Disney's hunchback and singing gargoyles.
Absolute silence is a must out here, as it was on opening night
of *Angels in America,* as it is before Jimmy Levine
conducts the orchestra like a traffic cop. And if we get lost?
We can find our way back to a Jacuzzi and yellow bath crystals,
to pot racks and spice drawers that help take the work
out of working in the kitchen. When we get home,
we can always go to Yuca, that Cuban upscale club for show-biz types.

MY SISTERS, THE OYSTERS

I feel like the striped Pacific bonito that can't stop swimming.
If it does, it suffocates. Next door, at the Portola Cafe,
people are eating my sisters, the oysters, at the Seafood Bar.
This is not like the Cocoplum section of Coral Gables.
I'm surrounded by clones of Mario Van Peebles: part man,
part machine, total weapon. I'm as free as a balloon let go
by a kid at a football game. If I need someone to play
flamenco guitar or a few percussionists to shake bead-filled gourds,
I can have it. If I want my house to have that slightly worn,
slightly edgy feel of industrial chic, I can find the exact right
architect who'll create virtuoso arpeggios in galvanized steel—
I don't have the money. I can only call for the complimentary,
in-home consultation. I can afford a one-time shot
at Le Cirque's lobster-stuffed sole, but why waste the bucks?
I'll settle for a flask of scotch and pizza home delivery.
A few Broadway shows, SoHo, MOMA and the Met.
Maybe Faneuil Hall, the North End and Filene's Basement.
Someday I'll get my packet of California wildflower seeds
as a hotel memento & I'll live in a place with a guard at the gate.
I'll travel far enough to experience impromptu parties
erupting in every piazza. But until I own a Caravaggio,
I must work and worry about fixing the natural gas furnace,
hoping the kids won't scale the walls after caffeinated sodas.
I'll dig out the old Halloween pumpkin face-carving kit
with its 9 carving tools and scraper/scoop & get started. Or I'll
take time off & search for the ultimate flea collar. Maybe I'll get lucky
like my sisters, the oysters, and be devoured in a gulp by a man
who'll take me to the 42 rooms and 100 townhouses
cantilevered into the cliffs of Monterey.

THE WINTER OF OUR DISCONTENT & OTHER SEASONS

This is the spring for rapid-fire pistol contests & Wall Street savvy,
not for visiting the great castle of Chambord. It's the summer
for figuring out if microbes are piggy-backing on imported oysters.
It's the fall for remembering that four-pointed bucks are being harvested
fast, and for jump-shooting ducks on the river. It's time for power-
positioning, not for automatic-pilot-command, remote control,
or voice-activated steering. I've already seen the yellow birch-snag
blackened by fire, and I've spotted the small striped maple
scarred by a moose's antler. Now it's time to bust my butt.
I want my poems to be less Marcia-centric, so I think I'll write
about Star Trek's Seska the undercover Cardassian spy. She had
a baby & stayed a little plump. She joined the health club.
To give her boobs a boost she worked her upper body with freeweights.
Her belly sagged so she did sit-ups on the Ab-Roller. To fix
her quads she jogged on the Po-Form at 5.0 for an hour a day.
She stocked up on low-cal decaffeinated drinks and Lean Cuisines.
For a while she looked pretty good. Not exactly like the latest Portrait-
in-Taffeta Barbie Doll. She still had those crinkly bumps and ridges
on her face, and the stringy red wig exposing the huge, bald forehead.
But she was closer than she'd ever been to looking like Barbie.
She'd never need to insure her legs for a million dollars,
and she'd never go to Elizabeth Arden for a manicure & facial,
but the point is, she *felt* good.Then she said screw it, and spent
days in bed eating crackers & Cheez Whiz. I'll bet old Seska
would just love to give me the Vulcan death-grip. . . . *Wow!*
That was hard work! I'd lie down on the Shaker pencil-post bed
and rest a little but I need a scotch before I make my next move.

Let's go outside and breathe in the greenery. It's a nice evening
with ground squirrels & blueberries. I've got at least a good half-
acre of roto-tilled ground, and a pond with cottonwoods.
It's a perfect night for tadpoles to nestle down in the mud. Or
for getting sucked through a wormhole into the Gamma Quadrant.

DOROTHY AND TOTO IN NEW YORK

Dorothy, scooped up by a tornado, plop—lands on the Fifth Avenue
doorstep of Eileen Ford's Modeling Agency, her make-up looking
like toxic sludge & her hair like kudzu swallowing a barn in summer.
Toto, a blind white mutt w/ black circle around his eye—who noses his way
through alfalfa, or hops up steps, turning left for the kitchen & his bowl,
without bumping into walls—cowers near Dorothy, his nerves
rattling like dice in a cup. The door opens & Dorothy learns the book-
on-your-head walk, the hip-swivel & hair-toss. She learns to hate men
who say, "You gotta call my agent when you get to L.A," or "Let's
get a cupp'la stogies & a pint bottle of Double Black Stout."
(Their charm is linear & superficial—more persona than personality—
except when undressed for success.) She forgets Kansas—her aunt's
purple Cabbage Rose wallpaper, raisin pie, & oakleaf lettuce—
her uncle's handmade bits & spurs and classic Don Dodge snaffle.
She forgets how easy it was to make worn-out boots into bird houses.
Once she preferred a good britchen to a crupper—a britchen keeps
the saddle from moving forward, but unlike a crupper, a britchen turns
the horse's entire hindquarters rather than just the tail. Now she forgets
what a crupper is, & also the ten-pound leeks at the county fair. A long way
from clotheslines in the back yard, she's all chit-chat, cognac,
weekend tee-shots over the dune—all Tony Bennett at Carnegie Hall,
& politically correct faux-fur. She's all pate imported from Paris,
stone crabs from Miami, violin concerts in glass-enclosed pergolas,
& purebred Irish Setters. Alas, poor Toto! He sniffs Central Park
benches (& grassy patches like home) for Dorothy but can't catch
her scent, masked by Paul Mitchell hairspray & Coco Chanel. Toto—
a shaggy mutt so far from his alfalfa & his bowl, so far from his back
yard in Kansas with the smell of laundry flapping on the line, & sunflowers
that, unbeknownst to him, turned their heads to follow the arc of the sun.

MEDUSA, 1996

It's hardly a secret. I've persisted through investigations,
convulsions, and near extinctions. I've worked for a living,
stood stock still, taken the brick wall personally, kept my head up,
navigated from here to there, as my bloodvessels constrict in the cold air.
I've lost the keys, gotten splinters, had grapes in my mouth,
hung laundry. And yet the underside of a leaf can still surprise me—
as if I've just been knocked breathless by a cathedral-shaped silence.
If it weren't for such moments I'd be standing here half-asleep,
wild-haired, as the dawn begins again from scratch
to build the stage sets—the houses and streets where we live—
exposing the naturally hidden places. But what are the facts?
That Saturdays are littered with wasted hours? That wet rags,
like razors, have no capability of feeling a wave of love?
That the night isn't like a mute swan? That flowers are growing
in small undisturbed places in the imagination where all things doze?
Under pressure this gruesome reverie will grow a trifle warmer.
As it was on the first day of creation. I can see too much,
even the wrinkles on the shirt of an explorer who steps on a thorn.
It could happen to you. You might one day wake up and find that your
mind is fractured and that the light streaming through its cracks
is quick to fall on slights of any sort. Like me, you could live in fear
of someone touching your sleeve. I've squatted for too long
among the flowers. Now it's time to wobble through the world
looking past the whitewash. I've got a blueprint and tactics. I've got
excuses, impertinence, signatures, threats. My suitcase is packed
full of whims just in case the mayor of great ideas should interrogate me
under the ceiling fans. But what if nothing should happen? What if
something as simple as a chat with you, dear reader, should cause the stars
to suddenly dish out pain? And how do I know that this means of transport
called the body isn't tailored to fit an enemy who has forgotten me?

STONE WORSHIP

I could have spent an entire lifetime laughing in despair
but instead I worshipped a black stone. It fell from the sky
into the bed of iris near the barn. I can't fathom this invisible
sluggish brain we call God, and so I worship a stone, a black stone.
I'm daring to harness a darker truth, to let the temple of my body
be an oasis in which a stone can become a living legend, a bundle
of nerves—Here I am, chatting again, as we're walking down
Worry St. past the Accident Museum to Division St. where
you'll go one way and I'll go another. I know that you're a self-
evident fraud, and yet compared to you, the rest of the alter-egos
are a bunch of myopic pinheads, sleazeballs, eccentric gurus
that won't shut up. I'm still fuming from the spewed-out lies.
Even a rare bird such as yourself should understand. This isn't
a world of free refills and fully-furnished office suites.
This is a world in which you can gather wildflowers and find
yourself catapulted into the headlines. This is a world
in which the rain's falsetto voice isn't appreciated, a world
in which the books we read, the clothes we wear, and the food
we eat are lapsing into history. It's not a pretty thing
to be wiped out by dust in which nothing grows but footprints.
Because that's what history is. You don't believe me? Then
what about the famines, plagues and epidemics that have been
reduced to nothing but a leaflet under your hotel room door?
What about the intense and hungry-looking stars? It's not as if
they were born yesterday. Better to worship a black stone,
better to cruise the internet without seat belts, better to
drink so many cups of coffee that you're wired like satellite TV,
able to pick up signals from anywhere in the universe but here.

TWO FAIRY TALE FIGURES GIVE ME ADVICE

1. *Notes from the Tower*

You don't know why, but the cracked shell of a walnut
is just as frightening as twelve hands holding torches in dark hallways.
You're afraid to think about a castle approached by knights
who haven't eaten for days, a cottage owned by a woman named Katya;
also the knife that causes blood to change into walruses, as it flows
into the sea when a father cuts his daughter's hands.
To save yourself, think of small things: hair on the upper lip
of an old woman who said: "Between you and the singing water
is seven years' journey. Find the garden of mother Ogress.
She sleeps for seven years and is awake for seven years. . . .
Take this road—take this thread and pull everything through
the eye of the needle: birds, sky, field, everything down
to the last blade of grass trampled by the knight's horse,
down to the last tree, next to the golden cage in which the lark sings:
'I'm tired! Isn't there someone who will say to me, "Rest!"
Isn't there someone who will say to me, "Sleep." Isn't there someone—
isn't there someone. . . .'" Is your body visible through your dress?
Are your bones visible through your body? Are your nerves,
spreading this way & that, visible through your bones?
If only you could find the key. Twenty flights of stairs between you
and the waterfalls of ice. Twenty flights between you
and the bridges made of cattle skulls. If someone wearing gloves
seizes the handkerchief with the three drops of blood on it
& throws it into the flames, you'll be saved.

2. *The Magic Broom*

Walk out into the fields without looking behind you.
If you see an owl tearing a rabbit with its claws,
close your eyes. A woman will pluck a golden hair from her head
and throw it to the ground. It will make a twang
like the vibration of a guitar string. She's not your real mother.
Beware of snakes living by the roots of trees.
When your cap falls off and you are visible again,
snakes will surround you. Hit them with sticks.
They'll tie themselves in knots, hissing as they disappear.
You'll recognize your real mother by the black thread
in the shoe of her right foot. You'll recognize your father
by his questions: What has one eye, an overcoat of polished steel,
and a tail of thread? What has four feet and feathers,
but is not alive? What walks without feet, beckons
without hands, and moves without a body?
Don't answer. Otherwise, he'll say, "I have eyes of flame,"
and your clothes will light on fire. You'll be condemned to roll
over and over in the dust until the last spark goes out,
and that could take years. Take this scarf, unroll it,
and a river will appear between you and your father.
If he crosses, take this hairbrush, shake it, and a forest will grow.
If he follows your tracks, draw a chalk circle,
and wait for him to step inside it. Then wave this handkerchief,
and the circle will become an island in the middle of a lake.
Now you can walk home. If you want to stay fatherless, though,
carry this broom—to sweep away each footprint behind you as you go.

WHY I HANG OUT WITH NERDS

When I'm with skinny guys who wear thick glasses
I feel like Marilyn Monroe, even though in most contexts
I'm more like a hippie Donna Reed. In a few cases—
in a dingy neighborhood bar, say, with pool tables
and a couple of hairy guys with skull/snake insignias
on the backs of their black leather jackets, I'd be considered
a preppie Janis Joplin. In Hollywood, of course, I'd be nobody
or a gorgeous Wicked Witch of the West. With violet contacts
& dyed black hair, I could pass for a garish younger cousin
of Elizabeth Taylor. If you looked only at my thighs and hips
after liposuction, you'd think I was Cindy Crawford,
and if I got breast implants, then maybe from my waist to my neck,
excluding my arms, I'd be Joan Collins. If you take the small section
of neck that is left after cancelling out Crawford and Collins,
you've got Lauren Bacall! If I had calf implants and a few ounces
of flesh surgically removed from the backs of my knees,
and you cancelled out everything *but* the knees and calves,
I'd be mistaken for Vivian Leigh. If you were to stare *only*
at the mole on my shoulder and imagine a cheek in place of that shoulder,
you'd think I was Madonna. If you removed all of me except
for the knuckles of my left forefinger, I could pass for Katherine Hepburn.
If you were to pull a *hair* out of that knuckle, place it next to a hair
pulled from one of Grace Kelly's knuckles, and if you were to compare
those hairs, you'd think that Grace Kelly & I were identical twins. . . .
Would a guy take me out to a sausage and egg breakfast at McDonald's,
or to a tuxedo dinner at Maxim's? In the case of McDonald's,
I'd be like the Wicked Witch of the West with Cary Grant, or Janis Joplin
with Clark Gable. But in the case of Maxim's, I'd be like Grace Kelly

with Lon Chaney, or Lauren Bacall with Peter Lorre. But what if
Lorre were replaced by Humphrey Bogart? Who would be several notches
above Lauren Bacall? If he were to look only at my thumbnail,
Bogart might fumble slightly, lighting my cigarette at Maxim's,
a rose petal falling from his white lapel into my glass of champagne.

KRIYA

—a Sanskrit word meaning action
"... a spiritual emergency or surrender.
I always think of Kriyas as spiritual seizures. ..."
—Judith Cameron

Where in the world do you want to go?
My fragmented soul has 5,000 locations world-wide.
Some pieces are in hard-to-get-to places like Ushuaia
or Lahad Datu. But many have turned up in larger cities
like Caracas or Santiago. Others are scattered in the provinces
of Kalimantan and Shikoku. A few have collected
in the Andes near Merida and Valeria. I'm tracking down
the endangered ones on Tierra del Fuego. There's no way
I can save the last three or four in Hong Kong. I've read books
on the care and feeding of souls & they've got a lot of nerve
to think they know anything about the specific problems
I'm having with *my* soul. The splinter-groups are hungry.
It's pizza night. How does home delivery work?
In Bhutan it's a long trek up the Himalayas, and pack-
mules are infested with leeches. Also, the more fragments
that evolve into self-sufficient mini-souls awaiting promotion,
the more they speak different languages. What if they ask me
how to say *mwezi* in Shuar or *namaste* in Dzongkha?
I wish they'd all come home to the U.S.A. But then they'd probably
be too linked together. They'd all want to go to the same mall
or to the same matinee, where they'd all converge at once
at the ticket window. ... If you must know,
my problems have turned me into a dazed couch potato.
I drink a lot of Sprite and channel surf satellite TV.
My soul likes to watch so many different programs at once
that channel surfing is the only way I can stay in touch.

POETS ANONYMOUS

I checked myself into the *Flowers of Evil* rehab center & didn't
write for a year. I was fine until I saw two red ants carry an inchworm—
one's got head, one's got tail—& now I 'll confess to my fellow
poetryholics at tonight's meeting. They'll say, "Just get out the ol'
Cordless Insect Disposal Vacuum and suck 'em up"—but one's got head,
one's got tail, & they're trekking up a long winding road (forsythia
sprig), lugging a bulbous, green, bile-excreting tube of flesh, heave ho,
heave ho. . . . See why I can't miss tonight's poetry *un*reading,
where we give each other gold stars every time we hear a phrase like,
"Last fall, I ripped out orphans & planted a dark purple river of iris,"—
& resist writing about it? If someone spots a sign for the First American
Knife Throwers Alliance National Championships & doesn't start a poem,
we clap—even louder for someone who, in an airport, hears over the
loudspeaker, "Mr. Gator, Al Gator, please pick up the courtesy phone,"
& then *un*hears it. (Last week, X confessed that it's tough to *un*see a sky
that looks as if it has been brushed with a coat of buttermilk white, then
hushed with a light double sponging of peach and pink.) We clap softly
for an erasure of, "We've zigzagged up the creek bed, past spiky lupines,
under the shade of cottonwoods, & now we'll canter all the way
to Mexico!" One lady says, "I daydreamed that my dog was typing letters
to Santa Claus, asking for bones & frisbees, & I had to call my sponsor."
Awwww—the audience sighs. A man who almost wrote about
his hard day slinging wisecracks at the office while Timothy Leary's ashes
orbited in space took a cold shower instead. *Bravo!* I tell the ants &
inchworm (one's got head, one's got tail, heave ho, heave ho) story.
Arrrrg, a fellow junkie shouts, *Who'd want to write about that?*

THE AMISH ON ROLLERBLADES

We're witnessing right now, *this minute,* the Amish
learning to rollerblade. They won't accept the bicycle
as a way to get around, but rollerblades are the closest thing
to their own two feet. Yesterday they were worried only about thin,
shelly hoof-walls and saddle racks & today they're looking into
Rollerblade's fusion line, with adjustable brake height
and heel lock. They're beginners, so they're practicing
how to fall by skating over to soft-looking patches of grass
& learning to *roll* rather than *slam* as they hit the ground.
Just yesterday I was raising black mollies in a jar separate from
their mothers who would eat them & I was catching garter snakes
before they shimmied between the garden wall's stones.
My red slider turtle sat all day in his bowl on the island with
the plastic green palm tree, and I rescued baby moles from drowning
in our flooded basement. Then I took a hairpin turn.
A door opened and I entered the world of Giorgio Armani
& Ms. Galaxy the fitness champ who is selling Hypergrowth formula.
I found Gary Kasparov playing chess against IBM's super-
computer, Deep Blue, that can analyze 200 million moves a second.
Now there's a 500 million dollar business mixing eggs
harvested from a woman's ovaries with sperm in a Petri dish.
I want to go back & hear my aunt say, "You have no business
in the dining or living room except to practice the piano." I want to hear
my uncle say, "Cook those quail quickly or you might as well use them
for badminton shuttlecocks." I want to walk a hardwood ridge with
my cousins & look for turkeys. I miss the old sagging barbed-wire fence
and the whitetails flicking their ears as they graze. I want to go back to my
childhood where the Amish aren't rollerblading. But now they're learning
to jump curbs. They're swivelling their hips & keeping their elbows tucked
to their sides as they slalom down hills, their beards & hair flying.

AN INVITATION TO NEW YORK

Let's fly through skies clogged with Lear Jets & look for a Ramada,
where we can sit in the rat-infested gardens & talk. We can always bring
our eel-skin jackets in case Hell freezes over & we feel the chill.
Let's kick up our heels and buck our way like a couple of studs
down Broadway, to the ladies-wear collection at Saks,
a couple of frisky stallions nosing the slips and panties.
We're hot, our veins containing Arabian blood for boldness
and speed. Let's look for dressage enthusiasts whose hips sizzle
as they walk. Or slog down a couple of Tequila-shooters
and do a bar crawl. Remember back seats of Chevies
when broads both loved & hated the 8-handed octopus-creature?
It'll be even better than that! We've got the best muscles
anybody's ever seen, multidimensional biceps and quads,
splitting into perfectly-sculpted veiny bulges as we flex.
We'll find those girls who are doing the *Best Built Babes* video
& take them out for Triple-Ginseng-Root sodas and burgers.
We'll put on our Hot Bodz Hi-Tech Supplex Vests & cruise.
Let's get out our hand-held electronic trigger-point finders
for inflammation detection & acupuncture those babes—
then go down to the Zippo & Knife Gallery. That forged L-6 blade
bit into the seasoned oak with ease, but I'd rather get a Texas Bowie.
I've taken my boa to a chiropractor who'll massage its spinal column,
smoothing out an irregular flow of nerve impulses, and I'm ready to go.
I've ordered my rifle case & my laser optic targeting system.
I've studied *Stock Challenge & Portfolio Alert*. I've got 5 grand
to invest *for real*. After 10 years of beating the S&P, I'm ready
to *splurge*. So let's make that trip & buy a Blockbuster Bucktool—
voted Overall Weapon of the Year. Then we'll go home & help
our wives plant the sweet peas & Mikado roses.

FAST LANE

Down at the Express Mortgage Center, they're sipping Java
and wondering if they've won the grand prize:
a General Electric kitchen appliance. It's easy to enter
a sweepstakes, but not so easy to get your 24 free
petit-fours from Swiss Colony, or to build a classic plant-
container-size pergola in less than an hour. Back in the 70s
all you had to do was jazz up Grandmother's damask.
I downed Quaaludes, got ripped on weed, and still carried four
plates at a time at Dino's, but I'm not sure I could've handled
today's cliché pastels and faux folklore Santa Fe look, or the $730
Jill Sander stretch pants. I might have gone for the cashmere/wool blend
tweed sweater designed for Barney's private-label line.
But mainly I thought about the thin eggshells caused by DDT.
I didn't know people were already waiting to *need* Tiffany lamps,
and the redesigned 1996 Mercedes Benz with door-mounted air bags.
I only knew that Elvis had listened in utero to his mother Gladys's
gospel singing in church. Now Warhol's dead, and everybody's
downshifting after a day in the fast lane. A few brave souls are taking off
for griz-country with the NASA-inspired portable fridge
that replaces the ice chest *and* doubles as food-warmer, the same
people who know that plastic worms are passé, and that versatility
and big tackle boxes are key. The way camping was in the old days,
Larry and I should've qualified for martyrdom by midnight
with our battered tent and Chef Boyardee Ravioli. Today
it's best to stay at home and paint eyes on lipless crankbaits,
oil the Zebco, or play dime-a-point cribbage after learning
that backing a boat trailer down a slick launch can be tricky.

I should've stayed back there with Larry in our micro-
waveless kitchen with the pink shag rug. We were happy then
drinking scotch and singing the Dead's *China, cat, sunflower.* . . .

—in memory of Larry Levis, 1946-1996

I'LL NEVER BE JOANNA

Buy the Furr's frequent shopper card, & you could win two days
at the Bob Bondurant School of High Performance Driving,
a run with bulls in Pamplona, or a North Pacific whale-spotting tour—
I listen to the radio. Then Joanna & I eat buffalo burgers, visit galleries
& see a spiral of butterflies—a swallowtail xeroxed 26,645 times,
each copy cut out, soaked in tea & glued to a wall. Also a woman's torso
made of thousands of minnows glued together in wavy rows, as if
still swimming—I wouldn't be happy crafting top-of-the-line pond yachts
that duplicate *actual* yachts from keel to mast, down to mahogony decks,
& hemp rigging. So why not let my refrigerator fill with dead minnows?
Why not xerox butterflies? Why not collect zebra leg-bones,
glue them to the ceiling & let them dangle over Grecian columns
adorned with monkey skulls hollowed out & filled with eggs?
When I write poetry in the middle of the night—I'm talking sweat,
flashes of light, & queasy cartoon figures that get transported
to other dimensions where they gain special powers for short periods
of time (the goal is to rescue the Dream Fly from the evil Swagman)—
I almost know what it would be like to chase fires, wrestle alligators,
or follow a minstrel show—i.e. what it would be like to be a Japanese
zoologist in 1958 who has just trawled a 40-armed octopus (a cone shell
can kill by it by injecting venom with a radular tooth almost as thin
as a hypodermic needle), or what it would be like to *be* the octopus.
But I'll never grow back a lost arm. I'll never eject ink in the shape
of my own body, then shoot away, turning pale. (I'll never adopt
a Japanese taboo against organ transplants, or paste butterflies to a wall.
I'll never be Joanna—with her pink pit-bull & passion for mustachioed
Yugoslavian ship captains)—I'll be me, with a frequent shopper card,
standing in a check-out line at Furr's, having just won a free flight
w/ a cargo of human eyeballs destined for patients in New York.

CHINESE BOX

Whenever my grandmother quoted Corinthians & said that the body
is a temple for the spirit, I thought of a Chinese box & the secret
panels that make it difficult to open. What if my spirit
took a walk, & came home to locked doors? And if I died?
Would my spirit know how to boil water or cook an egg?
Would it count out the proper change? My spirit would be dumbfounded
upon finding that, beyond the backyards safely tucked in by fences &
plenty of empty space, are worlds with *no* space—dark corners
in stairwells, where rats multiply and a hairy spider floats down
a thread to land on your face. My dumb spirit knocking on doors,
its knuckles flying through wood without making a sound, stumbles down
streets calling my name, while I—much too deep underground
to help it (much too far away to shout, "Did you wash carefully behind
your ears this morning?"), my voice muffled by pillowy purple coffin silk
& wormy dirt piled over me—must let my spirit haunt the streets
& sleep by the river, where it can hope *at least* to slip into the body
of a drowning man it can save. . . . Even if my spirit *could* find me—
by evaporating into a wisp of gaseous thought and condensing into a thin
layer of sweat upon my body, it wouldn't enter me—my body's
doors shut & concealed by moon-bridges & dragons breathing fire.

FOUR SIGNIFICANT CHILDHOODS

1. *Agatha Christie*

Mosquitos slept on the mauve walls of our hotel bedroom,
and my brother said, "Chimneys in Paris are quite
different from chimneys in England." I was homesick
for our raspberry garden, and the cake with sugar icing
& four candles. A red spider scurried across my plate,
and mother said, "It's a lucky spider, Agatha, a lucky spider
for your birthday." We moved & I practiced my French:
un chien, une maison, un gendarme, le boulanger.
My brother told me that French babies come in a doctor's
black bag whereas English babies are brought by the nuns.
I cut pictures out of old magazines and pasted them
into scrapbooks of brown paper. I bit my brother's finger
and realized I'd never have what I wanted most—
naturally curly hair, brown eyes, & the title of Lady Agatha.
We played the game of schoolmaster, & I'd shout:
"What year was the needle invented? Who was Henry VIII's
third wife? What are the diseases of wheat?"
One day the horses arrived & we zigzagged up a path
as our guide picked daisies for me to put in my hatband.
He caught a butterfly and pinned it to my hat. "Pour la
petite mademoiselle," he said. Oh the horror of that moment!
The wings still fluttered. I wept and couldn't stop.
I'd been thinking about the dollhouse furniture, left
at home, and the miniature family with porcelain heads
and sawdust limbs. Mother had fixed with glue a small black beard
and mustache to the face of the father, but none of that mattered now.
I wanted to disappear—just like the cat I'd seen that morning—

it walked between wine glasses on a cafe table, & without breaking
a thing, curled up, & fell asleep, suddenly invisible, its white fur
blending into the white linen cloth. It's the way sometimes,
walking in the woods, I'll say, "This is Agatha talking to herself."
Then I'll see a story unfolding. I'll know exactly what Maud
will say to Alwyn, just where the stranger will be standing,
and how the dead pheasant figures in, causing Maud to think
of an incident long forgotten. I'll rush home to the page, feeling
almost invisible, like the white cat. And the words will all be *there*.
It started that day as I wept and wept. I said to myself:
"Agatha is riding a horse, a flapping butterfly pinned to her hat"—
as if Agatha were someone else, & the weeping stopped.

2. Beatrix Potter

Before Jeremy Fisher Frog wore a macintosh
& shiny galoshes, or fished with a line of white horse-
hair, and before he sat on a lilypad, eating a butterfly sandwich,
the rain trickling down his back; & before Peter Rabbit
squeezed under the gate of McGregor's garden, only to catch
the brass buttons of his blue jacket on the gooseberry net,
I was no one, or just a girl wearing white pique starched frocks
and cotton stockings striped like zebras' legs. At tea time
I'd wait for the farm boy to stagger up the carriage drive
with his milk cans, or I'd sit under the green fringed table cloth
as Grandmamma gave me gingersnaps out of a canister.
I'd wait for Mr. Wood to bring his pocket handkerchief
filled with two dozen buff-colored caterpillars. Set loose,
they'd crawl up his shoulder & into his gray hair.
Later, my brother and I studied birds. I painted a dead
yellowhammer, its feet in the air, its head tilted back,

the sparse tail feathers picked clean by a cat. Sometimes,
we'd skin dead rabbits & boil them, saving the bones.
We'd stuff bats, stretching & pinning the wings to a board
after we'd taken measurements: length of head, body, tail,
humerus, radius, femur, tibia, pollux, and claw.
For my art teacher, I painted a still life of a pineapple
but couldn't resist including Judy, my pet lizard,
who later laid an egg— The embryo wriggled for hours,
its tail curled twice, its big eyes staring through the brown,
transparent shell. Then it died. The stare was like the stare
of the dolls in *The Tale of Two Bad Mice,* after Hunca Munca
and Tom Thumb have raided the red brick dolls' house,
after they've smashed the plaster ham and tossed the fish
into the kitchen's crinkly paper fire that won't burn,
or like the stare of the glass eyes that fell one day from a shelf
as I dusted the bone-cupboard where my brother and I
kept our collection of British mice. Skeletons broke,
& eyes scattered across the floor. For hours I mended bones,
as the blackness of each pupil seemed to draw everything into its gaze.

3. *B. F. Skinner*

When I was four, I stole a quarter from my grandmother's
purse, and my father took me to a lecture about Sing Sing.
The slides showed prisoners, in black & white stripes, splitting
rocks with sledgehammers. In those days, I was still afraid
of the grocery store where tarantulas might be hiding in the bananas,
and I thought the cat sleeping in my bed would put its face over my
face & inhale the life out of me. I'd rollerskate with a key
tied around my neck, my skates clamped to my shoes, or call
my brother "Honey" as we rode our bikes up Grand Street.
We'd circle the pond, afraid that dragonflies would sew

our lips shut. Or we'd look for quicksand—like Captain Marion,
the Swamp Fox, we wanted to escape from the British.
In *The Trial of Mary Page,* a movie we saw at the Hogan Opera House,
the retina of a murdered man was developed like a photographic plate
to show the person he was looking at when he died.
My brother died, staring at no one. On the way to the funeral,
I noticed that hoboes in the glen west of Susquehanna were heating
beans in tin cans just like the pictures in the funny papers.
And everyone had gathered, as usual, by the dam to watch huge sheets
of ice fall over the edge into the roiling water below—as if
my brother's death meant nothing, as if we were being paid back
for catching eels with our bamboo poles & cutting them up
after hitting them with baseball bats. I can still picture my brother & me
sledding on our Flexible Flyers, or jamming toothpicks
into the neighbor's doorbell. I wake up thinking he's still alive.
One day, in my office, a pigeon flew through the open window
& landed on my desk as I talked on the phone. I slipped
my fingers over its feet, pinning them down, its wings flapping.
For weeks, I taught it to play a single tune on a toy piano.
On the day my brother died, we saw trained pigeons at the state fair.
Smoke billowed out of a miniature cardboard building. A pigeon
poked its head out of a second-story window. Wearing red hats,
others pulled a tiny fire engine. With their beaks they propped
a ladder against the building. And the pigeon in the window was saved.

4. *Lana Turner*

Before I auditioned for the Major Bowes Amateur Hour
and sang "The Basin Street Blues," my father shot craps,
hit a winning streak, and stuffed the bills into his left sock.
They found him slumped against a wall on the corner of Mariposa
and Minnesota. He'd been bashed in the head with a blackjack

& his left foot was bare. At the funeral they asked,
"Do you want to kiss him goodbye?" I touched his hand,
& it didn't feel real. I couldn't cry. Later, Johnny Stompanato
held a gun to my head. We'd found a huge iguana—green
against the red pillows of the couch in our Acapulco suite.
He shot it, ordered champagne & caviar, put the gun to my temple
& said, "If you won't have me, you won't have anyone."
I sobbed the way Georgia does in *The Bad and the Beautiful*
after she's betrayed and drives through blinding rain. Actually,
they had big buckets, sponges and hoses, and the car
was propped on planks & springs. To cry, I thought of sad
things: my father's dead, waxy hand, and my mother's lie
about the lady wearing long white gloves. We lived near the tracks
in Wallace, Idaho. I was three. We'd sit in the yard, watching
trains. Once, a woman wearing long white gloves waved to me,
and Mother said, "Wave back, Honey. That's your *real* mother."
I didn't know what was real. It's like the *The Sea Chase*,
where the audience can't see John Wayne's ear infection,
the left side of his face swelling up. Or the twenty-six takes
in *Ziegfeld Girl* for one final drunken tumble down the stairs.
Before I touched my father's hand, I thought he wasn't really dead.
He was just lying there, faking it. He was too dressed up, like the men
who would ask me to dance, later in Rio, wearing perfumed ether
on their handkerchiefs. Then I touched his hand & realized
he was gone. I hadn't yet sipped my coke at the Top Hat Cafe
or worked after school, wrapping presents at a ladies' wear shop.
I wasn't "the sweater girl," who walks down the street
of a southern town in *They Won't Forget*, & I still wanted
my father to teach me how to tap dance for the Elks Club shows
in Wallace. But his eyes were closed. He'd never see my future,
or the producers building a river town for *Green Dolphin Street*.
He'd never see the climactic scene: the river rising, washing us away.

THE MOOD MUSEUM

1. *Depression*

A knock at the door, and there it was—Depression,
the corners of its mouth turned down in disapproval.
I said, "Excuse me. I've got dishes to do.
If you want to borrow something, a cup
of doubt or agony, you'll have to go elsewhere."
And it said, "If you think you can get away without noticing
the little black patches of shadow everywhere, you're mistaken.
You can either officially quit living, or I'll fire you.
You can suffer my condition marked by irreversible
mental deterioration, or you will forever be banished by the stars.
Would you rather shed your image and look more like me,
or become invisible so that you can see through yourself?"
"Go away," I said. The next day it was back.
"Already the voices inside you are cancelling each other out," it said.
"Even though you're making an effort to look innocent,
you are corrupted by waves of envy and nausea.
Fear and dread are rooting themselves at the base of your skull."
The next day, its pain was still with me, like a last note vibrating
on the strings of a harp. An anxiety serving no purpose
shuttled back and forth between my childhood and adulthood.
I was the inventor of misguided thoughts. I gazed
into my own interior, memorizing details—tables set for one,
and nothing but candles for illumination. I worried
that even the gray rain would leave me, due to its private set
of convictions. Maybe the sky had an airy, uncluttered look
because it was dreaming of my absence. I needed help.

I was an idle onlooker, while all around me flowers and trees
were giving me me suspicious looks. Were the saints applauding
my madness? The stars didn't owe me anything,
yet I kept feeling that they should pay me back. But for what?
I stood naked in front of the mirror so long that I saw
what I looked like before I was born: I was invisible,
like an accumulation of messages passing briefly through DNA,
a shadow passing through my parents' ability to get on each other's nerves,
or a gesture that hadn't yet expressed itself in terms of someone's hands.
I'm wondering, why do the unborn cross the existential divide into life,
breaking away from the oneness of light? Don't they know
that death will later retrieve them? Let me stay. Let me live here
in the wake of this starlight that will never forgive me!

2. Fear

"We borrow sadness and joy to find out what it's like
to be human. We laugh and cry at the wrong times,
caught in the crossfire of human emotions we don't understand.
Our tears shatter and bleed. For us there's no such thing as regret.
This body is only temporary, but I love the way skin and bones
pull me down to earth. Can I turn your fear into a chair?
I need something to sit on." An exotic vein bulged in the angel's forehead.
Had it come all the way across the cold squares of the calendar
just to share its secrets?—In the hierarchy of angels,
where exactly did this one fit? Was it asking for trouble?
It said, "Why don't you take my wings mottled by sunlight.
Now that the sky and its distances are accessible to you,
go ahead and fly out of that body that has trapped you for so many years."
My awareness, which distanced itself, started to soar in ways I could not
exactly formulate. Every face I saw below reminded me of yet

another face, which reminded me of still another face. Every violet
shadow multiplied in the dying light until I saw odd configurations
at the bottom of things—on closer look, they were hieroglyphics
I could apprehend without deciphering. Complicated messages
from the universe were translated in the form of black squiggles
and letters. For the rest of my life I'd be carving them into stone.
When I came back, I heard the rain stutter. Nothing was the same.
The wind on the creaking stairs was filled with accusations.
Before I could defend myself, a door slammed its "Shut up!"
I was quiet. I celebrated the anniversary of silence.
I scrounged around the earth, looking for a little anesthesia.
Everywhere I looked, the clean boundaries between things
grew fuzzy as if to tell me that I was being held there by a trance.
My thoughts rattling their misconceptions in my head—
these were my songs. And though, like light, I saw through
the manifestations of sorrow before me—a few spotted doves
perched on a sagging telephone wire in front of my house,
where all afternoon a lone shutter banged against the wall,
having come loose during a rainstorm of my tormented feelings—
I had trouble speaking. I waited for my angel to drift toward me,
its wings breaking through the surface of light, into the visible world.
I looked up. I kept pacing the ground. My hell was wrong.

—for Gerald Stern

3. *Anxiety*

The rain's nonsense syllables are locked in my head.
Am I really alive?
I wouldn't know just by breathing.
Small things happen to make me aware of it: gravel in my shoe,

or keys jingling in my pocket. . . .
When the sun splits the clouds it will clarify everything
except for the shadows that bother me.
I wear the shadows like sheep's clothing.
I keep my mouth shut.
My occupation is silence and doubt.
I'm looking for a fire escape. I'm hoping to slip unnoticed
with my suitcase out into the street.
But I'm worried that the sky will spot me if I run.
My mind is revving too fast
like an engine smelling of diesel.
The rain utters its keynote address,
and tomorrow the sun will want to interview me
in its harsh light. What should I do?
My worries objectify themselves into a leak in the roof
and a broken shutter banging against the house.
I open the refrigerator to find that my sour feelings
are milk gone bad. For hours I stare at the nervous and dizzy trees.
Then I pull myself together, go to a party, and chat,
a white silk rose in my hair. I say, "Nice to meet you!"
My self-hatred slips into a stranger's face
and stares back at me with its steely eyes and wild black hair.
I almost say to the face, "Your ears stick out. Ever think of that?"
At home I think, *Those trees will either die or go mad.*
I wish the wind would shut up.
It rattles the window like the intrusion of unwanted advice.
It crosses over the rage line,
beating the trees with its airy fists.
Maybe a secret inside of me has translated itself
into that crow clinging to a skinny branch.
The night is stealing things: a barn here, a field there.
Maybe a flock of sheep spirals into the heavens, sucked up by Time,

and nothingness is a mechanical genius.
Maybe Death is trying to talk me into backgammon
and will offer me a cocktail, saying, "Here, have a disease."
My glance drifting across the wallpaper
washes the floral designs with a tiny fraction of my ill will.
You asked for an explanation and all I can give you is
diagonal rain and my vintage record collection.
I can only give you forms to fill out and bills to pay.
It's God reaching down with a surgically-gloved hand
making a mess of this whole operation. I can't take it.
If the saints conducted seminars on timidity, I'd get an A.
The sky has no alternative address,
and morning will come, throwing its light
into obscure corners, undertaking the huge project
of the world's exposure. Until then, what should I do?

4. *Sloth & Torpor*

I won't get up. Not until morning stops this uncertain
giddiness and settles for a more straightforward daylight.
Somewhere, Death is rattling in its box, shaking with music.
Am I there too, materializing as a high, shrill note?
I'm at home with language in its big room of phrases,
but I'm also afraid that its subtle inferences might kill me.
What I mean to say is that the light's fervent impulses
are wasted on me. Or the night, seeking its private revenge,
won't let morning heal the breach made by the absence of light.
There are certain pockets of air in which my sadness
has become invisible matter nevertheless contained
by the intake of breath. I've given my replies.
I've named my silences. But what are their names?

How can I be expected to know when I haven't been informed
by the Big Blaze, the irrational occasion for the first pulse,
the first breath? We're here by accident—this morning
is giving me a lethal dose of lucidity. Luckily,
the sky at noon won't look at me anymore with such horror
that I will see myself as one of its major impediments.
I don't regard the sky as my chosen audience. I'd rather
address a substitute that isn't so wracked by useless grief.
Everywhere I look, the walls of flame aren't there.
And I don't know why. My friend, excuse me.
I've counted clouds until I've gone blind, in this dream
of staying alive in a place where everything
is put into question, even this voice—the voice of whatever I was
before I was born under the sign of a different logic, a different light.

5. *Ecstasy*

It's Fall. I walk around looking like everyone else.
But I've got decorative combs in my hair. . . .
I'm keeping these maples a secret.
They're doing me a favor, changing color.
I'm their guest. I won't be staying all that long,
but when I pluck a dying leaf, it's as if I'm holding
Time in my hands. Sadness isn't inoculating me anymore,
its chilly needle in my heart. The crows are gone,
their caws unintelligible like private jokes.
That was a close one. I almost didn't construct
infinitesimal distances to keep me aloof.
I almost didn't keep the clear boundaries
between things intact. But now I'm saved.

I've got my own breakable silence. It's there,
right now, in front of me, in the form of a man
who loves me. He's not saying anything,
but what a kiss! And my standards are high!
If you only knew what it was like, you'd want
to consciously work out your whole life
just to receive one such kiss! Is the afterlife
something like this, maybe—an extended moment
in which we are forced to live by a different logic,
as our bodies do? We've invented a new alphabet
in which touch exists on the border of speech:
On the other side of the border, time speeds up—
there goes my birthday—and we're already wondering,
are the mourning doves here to forgive and console?
We fall in love, marry, and the clock in the hall strikes five.
We fall away from our personal histories and scarcely notice
the small injustices. After years of scrutinizing each other's faces,
we still love what we see. We're saying that we're old.
We would rather shed our skins. We're saying that
the protean character of our souls will sustain us after death.
And why not? Do the maples care if their lost leaves
become documents proving that we were here? Thank goodness
the wind is shaking a little sense into those trees and we
have not fallen out of favor. I want to live here
no matter how difficult it is, on such short notice,
to take the place of the bulky shadows, no matter
how difficult it is to let the wind take away the leaves.
This kiss, I'm certain, is a form of erasure bringing us closer,
for a single moment, to the center of the earth's attention.

—for Murray

A MENAGERIE OF STRANGERS

1. *The Tunnel of Love*

We strolled all day through the Isle of Youth's arboreal
tunnel of love & spent evenings listening to the island's native
music, the *sucu-sucu*, a slow, countrified version of salsa.
We spotted tangerine-colored crabs & tree-scaling crocodiles.
We thought that seeing the walls & ceilings of caves carved
with red & black serpentine lines representing the celestial
calendar of the Ciboney Indians might give us a new perspective
& that goats asleep in the shade beneath the thatch-roofed
houses on stilts might relax us. We still came home to massive
PMS bloats & seas of Fudgesicle wrappers, to shaving cream
& black hairs in the bathroom sink. We argued about the rules
of tennis & about who played Hopalong Cassidy. When
our ferret ran away, we fought about whether or not to hire
Sherlock Bones, a pet detective who puts up mug shots
on telephone poles & has a data base of grooming parlors, vets,
& pet stores. We tried to cheer ourselves up by painting
the kitchen lime green, the cabinets canary yellow, & the closets
in mauve & blue stripes. We bought a chair shaped like a hand
& an Eiffel Tower hat rack. But we still looked at each other
& said, "You left the car windows open before it rained.
You forgot to take out the trash. *You're* the one who said that
Vietnamese Potbellied Pigs are housetrainable & don't grow big.
And now, look at him, snorting & drooling, occupying half
of the sofa." We thought that setting up targets in our backyard
to practice fly-casting might help us. We took up white-water
rafting & kyaking. But we argued about God and sex.

Finally we sold the chair shaped like a hand, & donated the pig
to the petting zoo. You packed your suitcases as I wept
in our green kitchen. Before slamming the front door, you shouted,
"You're so stupid you didn't even know who painted 'American
Gothic'!" "Yeah?" I said, "Before you met me, you didn't even know
the 13th president of the United States was Millard Fillmore!"
But you were already gone, your heels clacking down the walk.

2. *Homebody Blues*

It's October & my Christmas list is done. For Dad,
a Hammacher Schlemmer Nose Hair Trimmer. For Mom,
a Vehicle Positioning Parking Signal that beeps before you crash
into the garbage cans lining the garage's back wall. For my brother,
the Golf Fisherman that rakes the bottoms of pools for balls.
He quit his job & migrates up & down the West Coast in his van,
stopping at golf courses to snorkle the ponds. Business is booming.
Fifty million used balls are bought each year. Meanwhile, I'm
scrubbing tiles with a toothbrush and checking the fridge for rotten
apples & wilted lettuce. I deserve to ride a red double decker bus
through London to the Duke of Wellington's house where the tables
are set with Portuguese silver dinner service. I've planted the tulip,
allium and dwarf daffodil bulbs, sewn ghost costumes out of polyester
chiffon for the kids & made twig hair for the pumpkin. Why can't I take
a break & go to San Miguel Island to watch the sea-elephants mate,
or swim & sail in Curtain Bay, then eat lobster & drink Planter's Punch
on the beach? All I do for adventure is send away for a free squid ink
risotto & roasted sea bass w/ poached figs recipe, or listen to my Sound
Soother Relaxation System that masks harsh noises with four realistic
digitized sounds: North Woods, California Coast, Rain Forest,

& Tropical Cruise. How do people leave home for weeks without
worrying that the pink orchid in the kitchen will die? How do they know
they haven't left the coffee pot on? What if the roof leaks again
& the water stains on the Berber carpet get even worse? How
do they know that the mold behind the stove won't grow uncontrollably,
or that the fish/cigar/wet dog odors sprayed with Lysol won't come back?
Don't they hate to fly? On airplanes, only a third of the air is fresh.
The other two thirds is nothing but recycled breath of strangers.

3. *What Happened Next, Happened Fast*

When I last saw grandfather, he was getting Mr. Furball
ready for the handicapped class at the Big Apple Ferret Show.
He'd washed Mr. Furball with Ferret Glow Shampoo & deodorizer
with aloe vera and was using the Four Paws Tender Touch
slicker wire brush for ferrets. Never mind that Mr. Furball
had three paws. Grandfather had just come back from teeing it up
with some of the boys at the Australian Skins Tournament
for a skin worth six thousand dollars. When he got back,
he had a new square driver with a bright orange shaft & he showed me
all about swing-weighting & flex kickpoints while Mr. Furball slept,
caged & curled in his hammock. My grandmother cooked Texas Two-Step
Picante chicken. She'd joined the Doubleday Book Club to get the free
umbrella & tote bag and was already making Christmas decorations
in August. (One Egg Diorama ornament for the tree takes a large
white chicken egg, watercolor paints, spackling compound, a small
soft watercolor brush, reindeer moss, snippets of white or pale blue thread,
waxed paper, eight to ten inches of gold ribbon, twelve to sixteen cedar
seed pods, balsam fir cones, gold thread, cuticle scissors, tweezers,
white glue, cotton gloves, a bamboo skewer & a pint jar of sand.
You can see why she started early.) I'll miss my grandparents.

Why didn't they settle for a week at the Kahala Hilton, with its massive
cut-glass chandeliers, chintz couches & huge pots filled with Birds
of Paradise? Or maybe a junk-rigged boat cruise, complete with native
tapestries, porcelain, & carvings to remind guests that they're in Thailand?
Instead, they took an Alaskan brown bear hunting trip. They set down
their crossbows and wandered off to watch two cubs dig for squirrels.
An eight-foot bear lumbered out from behind the alders & stood there
stuffing blueberries into its mouth. They tried to crawl away on their hands
& knees through the bushes & mud, but then the bear saw them &
growled, curling back its berry-stained, rubbery lips. . . .

4. *Haven't We Met Before?*

You're the guy who recommended Renee's aromatherapy massage.
You had the Mickey Mantle commemorative baseball with display stand,
and the garnishing set including double melon baller & butter curler.
Didn't you raise tropical fish and phalyaenopsis orchids? Didn't your
Capricorn moon sextile your seventh house Mars in Sagittarius? No?
Then you're the one who told me to cut chines from a twelve-foot
oak flitch, to fasten the butts with flat-headed smooth-wire copper nails
and to do the final bevelling at the vise with a block plane, spokeshare
or rasp. You memorized Englebert Humperdinck's "There's a Kind of Hush
All Over the World." You scuttled far out on mudflats & huddled in wet
pit blinds surrounded by decoys, watching the flocks of new geese
pouring in from the north, & you knew the exact latitude and longitude
of your barstool. Or are you the one who said that my conventional
anti-freeze was full of tiny particles of silicates that wear down
the water pump seals? You sold me on the heavy-gauge Dynaflow
muffler & double weighted gasketless torque-tube manifolds. No?
Then you're the guy who said that if I visit the fly fishing club
on Chopaka Lake I should bring my own belly boat & DuPont Sealskinz

waterproof socks, and that if I go to Honolulu I should try the breakfast buffet at the Plumeria Beach Cafe. You *did* once judge the Working Dog group at the Lawrenceville show, didn't you? And we talked about the Amish tobacco farmers of Lancaster County. You took pilgrimages to Pennsylvania for cigar companies in search of the highest quality leaf, right? Or are you that plastic surgeon who zaps stretch-marks with a pulse-dye laser? Let me introduce myself. I'm _____. Who are you?

A SATURDAY NIGHT AT THE FLYING DOG

I was drinking Stoli with Helen & a young guy
tried to hustle me big-time. Really he'd just hitch-hiked
from Glenwood Springs and needed a place to stay.
No *way* anybody was going to follow me back to my place.
He was lot meaner & scruffier than I'd thought—around midnight
I started to sober up and could see it. When I split,
he did too. He "walked me" about half-way home,
and even though I told him over & over I was just *fine*
he wouldn't turn back. Finally I got scared & said:
"You know how wolves are territorial and pee everywhere
to set their boundaries? If you cross this line, you're *dead*."
I pointed to my feet, then bolted. I didn't want him to see a middle-aged
woman slip off her shoes & run like hell, but the moon was out.
I could feel him see me disappear, my purse and skirt flapping,
into a wall of spruces. I ran through an alley & no matter how
familiarly blue the columbines were, they froze in fear.
And aspen trunks looked fluorescent as if exposed to a blacklight.
The next day, Murray came back from New York.
After his shower, he put on his aqua & white-striped bathrobe.
His hair was white & curly as always, and his face had the usual tan.
He's got a little gold filling, a speck on a canine tooth that shimmers
when he smiles. I've never been so glad to see anybody in my life!
Today I've got to get to work dead-heading flowers. I've got to pick
the last few sprigs of thyme before the dog gets them—our Lab
also eats chives and he's splashing around, biting the water,
in his plastic swimming pool. I'm about to get up from the lawnchair,
when six evening grosbeaks flurry out of nowhere, a whirlwind
of yellow and gray surrounding the feeder. They're migrating

down valley! After a few seconds, they take off—
And floating down from the upstairs window is Murray's voice
saying, Marcia? Marcia! Where's the. . . . I look up, see his face & know
that *this* is it, our little territory of happiness, our wolf country.

BLACK PEARLS

On Lutheran Day in Arlington, Texas, born-again
baseball players speak in tongues & hand out religious tracts
instead of autographed photos. I feel so distant from them
that if I felt a bit closer, George Clooney, who in 1982
drove from Augusta, KY, to L.A. in a beat-up Monte Carlo
in pursuit of an acting career, would be my best friend.
And Roy Sawyer, curator of Charleston, South Carolina's
Medical Leech Museum, with its ornate bleeding bowls,
and 18-inch Amazon leeches fed on sausage casings filled
with stillborn pigs' blood, would be my second best friend.
My sisters & brothers would be Mexican zoologists crawling
the beaches looking for Kemps Ridley Sea Turtles, 120 years old.
And I'd be making a million dollars inventing liquid leather
insta-fabric while feeling desperate & homely,
like those Elizabethan women who plucked their hairlines
for higher foreheads, & drank dog urine for softer skin.
I'm a foreigner here. I'd like to teach the locals how to mix
martinis and lead nature tours, but I'm a tourist myself,
wanting to see everything—from a five-foot, pink Mississippi phlox,
to a six-foot striped canna from South Africa (which of course
makes one only more desperate than ever to own a variegated radish
with three-foot crinkly green leaves & white blotches).
Before I die, I'd like to see Polynesia's 500 pearl farms.
Beneath the placid blue waters of the lagoons, millions of black-
lipped oysters hang in mesh panels, nourished by tidal flows,
the pearls inside growing microscopically every day—black
pearls giving off a rainbow lustre. I'm closer to those pearls
than to the Texas Rangers baseball team chatting in the locker room:
"Noah? No, *Jonah* got barfed up on the beach at Nineveh."

EARTHLY LIGHT

Miracle seekers bring offerings of money, candy, and teddy bears
to the glass-topped coffin bearing the body of Miguel Angel,
a one-year-old who died thirty years ago of meningitis
and is dressed in the tiny soccer uniform of Argentina's champion team,
the Boca Juniors. If we need to believe in something, why not
believe in heaven, where the Safri Boys Band in fluorescent clothes
play reggae, as saints with portable vacuums strapped to their waists
suck up dust from the purple silk curtains, and on scaffolds drag
six-foot-long feather dusters across the plaster cornices—all
in preparation for tourists to help pay for the gazillion-dollar
restoration project. Heaven's a tear-down. Frankly I prefer
earthly light, bands of moss and water-washed stones.
I like the way this laceleaf pours over the retaining wall,
echoing the pond's waterfall. The good news is that peregrine falcons,
wearing tiny satellite transmitters, can be tracked all the way from Alaska
to Argentina. The bad news is we'll soon be watching Disney's
version of David shooting Goliath with a slingshot. And the Japanese
have beaten us to the microcar, as tiny as a grain of rice, complete
with 25 parts, including headlights and hubcaps. It can travel
up and down a matchstick. Every 12 weeks a new aquatic microbe
swims into San Francisco Bay. Now there are sponges, sea squirts,
and microscopic protozoa from Japan. The Chinese Mitten Crab
walks its hairy claws right into houses in Germany! The good news is
I grew up between a hardware store and a lumberyard. Back then,
if anybody had proposed painting the front door hot pink
and the exterior purple, to show off the orange trumpet roses,
we'd have laughed. If anybody had proposed buying Gucci loafers
with the signature horse bit, we'd have laughed. We wouldn't have laughed
at the bronze statue of B.B. King, holding Lucille, his guitar.
But we *definitely* would have laughed if anybody had said, "Did you know
that from our country estate windows, you can see the Pyrenees?"

A VACATION IN BOCA ISN'T RILKE

We're hanging out in our room at the Sands Hotel & Casino Beach
Resort in Boca Raton & it's funny. Once you've seen
one duo of chocolate chip cookies instead of mints
on your pillow at bed turn-down time, you've seen them all.
We might as well be at the Tanjung Aru in Kota Kinabalu,
except that pink & gray Java sparrows flutter past balconies
in Borneo. The same funky lizards do push-ups on the trees.
It's the same scotch & soda, same Sony TV. Not like Bimini
in the 60s—a hide-out for the Berrigan Brothers, with no
sightings of the new electric yoyo. Guys shot craps,
ate conch soup, and sticky burrs kept tourists off the beach.
A tiny sea-plane bounced away from Miami. No Hawaiian shirts,
cabanas or coolers. We rode around on black Raleighs,
not on comfort-oriented cruisers with moustache handlebars,
seven speeds, and a saddle that doesn't bite. In the 90s
you'd trade your ego for a drive in a 190-horsepower,
shift-on-the-fly, four-wheel-drive Passport EX.
You'd trade your unconscious for the newest fitted
high-buttoned tweed sport coat, so long as it has plenty of versatility
in or out of the office. You'd trade your superego
for a Dopp kit equipped with Coppertone 30, Gillette Anti-
perspirant Stick, and Binaca. You'd give away your id
for a great head of hair, compliments of Head & Shoulders—
your dandruff is taken care of and no one'll ever know
you had a problem. It won't work just to limey up your look
with long scarves and cotton-moleskin trousers. It won't work to add
a few military touches to your wardrobe—a slide-buckle belt
and aviator-style sunglasses. You're still the same
bunch of clowns we were in the 60s, except that a few more
poems by Rilke flew by us in the 60s, and Rilke could travel
so far back in time that he saw *trees rear up, not yet tame.*

A PORTRAIT OF LARRY WITH TROGONS

At first you can't spot a red & green trogon against
a background of deep green leaves & red berries.
It's also difficult to find the exact right words for poetry
when they're camouflaged against the background of speech,
newspapers, and T.V. If you were to see the trogon
against a white wall, you'd be dazzled by its brilliance. The same
goes for the right words when they're taken out of conversation
& placed into the unnatural habitat of poetry. If you train yourself,
you'll eventually see the trogons when nobody else can. . . .
Sorry, I'm too tired for this right now. It's midnight & my
18-year-old son took off for the East Coast today from our house
in Colorado, & he didn't take enough money or food.
He just finally called to say he's briefly stopped at a Ramada,
not to spend the night, but to use their hot-tub. He *also* told me
he's borrowed my credit card. I worry like crazy when he does
things like that! He'll probably get caught in the hot-tub and call me
in trouble with the desk clerk or he'll lose the credit card.
I can't blame him. He's sad right now because his dad,
the poet Larry Levis, has died. When someone you love passes away,
it's almost impossible to grasp the sheer darkness of it
against the solid blackness of death itself. Nick & I feel Larry
slipping away into the habitat of history, where too many names and faces
go blank. We've got to get him back. We've got to lock him forever here,
like a trogon, in the cage of our hearts, where he stands out.
But a trogon's natural instinct is to sit on a branch, deep inside
the green-leafed tree with the berries & hold perfectly still & upright—
its long slaty tail wavering ever so slightly in the breeze. Or
to rise & flap against a backdrop of white sky, where just as you try
to grasp the brilliant & quick presence of it, it disappears.

A WALK ALONG THE FOX RIVER

If someone buys a Bulgari watch that costs as much as a car,
& someone else walks along the frozen banks of the Fox River;
if the Birdsong Marina in Tennessee offers half-day boat tours,
& the state park naturalist describes how mussel-harvesting has developed
since Indian times; if Mary J. Blige, the queen of hip-hop, earns a rep
for her streetiness—combat boots & leather jackets—
& suddenly switches from dreads to French twist, from thigh-highs
to Christian Dior ankle-length dresses, from pierced eyebrows
to Cartier earrings & Estee Lauder flawless-finish make-up;
if she bows down & gives thanks to revolving gym-memberships and spa
cuisine—(no more Babe Ruth breakfasts: 18 eggs,
3 slices of ham, 6 pieces of toast, & 2 bottles of beer)—
what does that mean? Along the Fox River, there are no mango-
colored hotel rooms painted with wall & ceiling trompe l'oeil
scenes of Venice. You wouldn't want to be abed in full make-up
& nothing but ostrich feathers at a Budget Inn. If you worry
about the Australian stray cats killing the last woylies,
boodies, numbats, & potoroos; if you want to be your own
avatar & wear fuzzy ear-muffs & cartoon prints; if your
single desire is to open a window & find all of the terra cotta
domes and caramel-colored spires of Florence shimmering before you;
who cares? In the warp & woof of the modern world, if you decide
you're *you*—without the 100% Irish linen, risotto primavera,
stogies, chocolate truffles, & raku-inspired masks from Colombia—
you should take a walk along the Fox River & forget your hand-washable
Maurada lattice-design sweater w/ crochet overlay. You haven't applied
to Wendelstedt's Umpire School under the pseudonym "Bernie."
You aren't eating skewered chicken intestines & unhatched duck embryos.
You're walking along the Fox River. Wake up! You're *you*.

THE STAR SALESMAN

Romero Mendez sells maps of nameless stars, each one marked
with an X, & a document that says, you own _____.
(Fill-in-the-blank. You name your own star & he makes big bucks.)
The Hubble telescope recently pointed to one of the emptiest
parts of the sky, focused on a region the size of a pea
held at arm's length & found layer upon layer of galaxies.
I've payroll-clerked in a meat packing factory,
waitressed at El Diablo, made beds & cleaned toilets at Holiday Inn,
sales-clerked at clothing stores, written poetry, finished college &
graduate school, married, divorced, written more poetry, raised a son,
moved four times, remarried, written *more* poetry. . . .
What if I had sold stars instead, relaxed & smug, while astronomers
staring through telescopes, found more & more stars for me to sell?
If linguists could invent endless lists of new phrases, I'd speak
a language you'd understand only in part. The poem, a foreign object,
would stare back at you from the page, glistening with newness
and beauty, like an unnamed star I've sold you. But if
you chose not to buy it, what then? While you're sending away
for your free poster of antique pond yachts, or complimentary decorator
carpet-sample portfolios from S & S Mills, I'm still writing poetry.
I'm not laundering red-tailed black cockatoos, routing them
through New Zealand & then selling them for $20,000 each.
I'm not showing off by floating 3,000 meters up in a garden chair
strapped to 45 weather balloons. I'm not developing Leisure World
in Laguna Hills—a community of 18,000 that has 8 tennis courts,
14 security guards, a library, an auditorium theatre, a gourmet restaurant,
2 golf courses, & no wildlife. I'm writing poetry. Just think of this poem

as a mirror. You can look in it or not. You can search for the right
shade of lipstick or read this poem—play slots at the casino
or read this poem—rub linseed oil into your riflestock or read this poem.
If you've just bought a star, this poem is for you. Take it. It's free.

THE WORLD'S GREATEST ELECTRICIAN

At Hope Cemetery in Barre, Vermont, baby boomers
buy personalized gravestones. Mom & Pop stores
have been replaced by malls. Our cars are all alike.
Why shouldn't a man own a tomb topped with a black
granite light bulb and an epitaph that says, "World's Greatest
Electrician"? If he were any different and decided to buy
the "carpenter casket," a $19.95 instruction kit for a simple
make-it-yourself coffin that can double as a bookshelf,
armoire, hope chest, or coffee table, that wouldn't bother me.
But if I were to move to Pahrump, Nevada, which at first glance
looks like the perfect town for raising kids, and I later found out
that our man wasn't an electrician at all, but a teacher at Parhrump
Junior High who drops pencils & looks up girls' skirts,
that would bother me. If he turned out to be a Wall Street analyst
with 8 kids and a 190 lb. bull mastiff and lived in rooms
filled with heirloom furniture—fitted with washable slipcovers
and high shelves stacked with porcelain dinnerware only to be used
on Sundays—that wouldn't bother me. But if I then found out
that he was really an investor vulture, swooping down on hometown
factories, causing friends and neighbors to lose their jobs,
that would *definitely* bother me. But I'd turn my head away—
(no need to run for cover just because of dark circles from lack of sleep.
Just head over to the nearest Chanel beauty counter for a quick
cover-up)—because our man, the World's Greatest Electrician,
has plugged himself into a source of energy far greater than my own,
that propels him beyond the slings and arrows of outrageous fortune.
He can witness the decline of the fashion glove industry without flinching.

He doesn't get sidetracked by his travels—the cool dry Cypriot sun,
taste of wild greens, halloumi & deep fried taro root. He doesn't worry
that Polynesian coral reefs are being bleached & eaten away
by polluted waters. What does he care? He's already dead & content
under his black granite bulb that never lights up or burns out.

BODYSITTERS, INC.

—"I'm a ghost wanting what every ghost wants, a body."
—William Burroughs

I'm a ghost wanting what every ghost wants, a body—preferably
without arthritis, or mold/mushroom/birch/mugwort allergies,
heartburn, or yeast infections. I don't want to starve your body
by losing 5 lbs. in 5 days on the Slim-Fast jump-start plan, so if
you fit perfectly into a size 8 coral wool gaberdine suit by Oscar
de la Renta, don't put on any extra pounds before we meet.
No exotic tastes or beliefs please—if you eat wild hickory nuts
or honey ants plucked from the roots of a mulga tree—if you draw
crosses of beeswax on your forehead to rid yourself of your fear
or believe mosquitos originated when a bloodsucking giant's ashes
thrown to the wind caused each ash to fly, buzz, & bite, don't reply.
No rural Kentucky squirrel-brain eaters, or people from Dusseldorf
who put mustard on everything. No late-night-TV "prayer warriors"
cursing tumors & warts, or Captain Americas who play kazoos
& thunder machines in day-glo fingerpainted blacklit rooms.
No Tibetan Buddhist monks specializing in sub-baritone multiphonic
rhythmic chanting, or Neil Cassidy wannabees who hot-wire cars
& read Proust between dishwashing jobs & paper routes. And *certainly*
no bowstring hunters who can shoot an arrow through 10 inches of bear
hide & muscle. I'd prefer the body of an Armani-suited banker who
frequents charity balls & The Four Seasons, but if you're a shapely
housewife who cruises newspaper auctions in Topeka looking for yellowed
front pages to put behind glass with antique hankies or specs in shadow-
box arrangements, that's OK—as long as you don't *also* attend mass
twice a day. Are you seeking a genuine out-of-the body experience?
Call me. Come on over, unzip your carcass & float a while.

PSYCHIC FRIENDS NETWORK

You can hail a taxi on Madison Avenue, hit golf balls
down the middle of the fairway, sink your teeth into a pastry-nugget
laced with chocolate truffle or marzipan; you can crave sushi,
bowling, or *Madame Butterfly,* but you'll still feel a tidal tug
of sadness—as in the heartbreak of Merle Haggard's songs.
Good luck finding happiness writing poetry. (I'm an employee
of the Psychic Friends Network. I should have been an estate planner.
My astrological chart shows that between the ages of 21 and 25
I could've achieved financial success, but I didn't go to business school.
Jupiter & Uranus in the 7th house, squared by Neptune in Libra
makes me a poet/psychic.) What lasts is "The People vs. Larry Flynt,"
& the national debut of the $9 movie ticket. An ordinary potato,
transformed into a souffle seasoned with garlic & chives,
lands in a cookbook selling 100,000 copies, while this poem
could go extinct, like the Moth Orchid, or the Jamaican Rice Rat,
which did not survive the coming of the Europeans & *their* rats.
If it's not too late, after skateboarding: a frontside/bluntside to fakie
an old rail or backside/tailside, riding durby faster than hell—
(practice more heelflips & handrail tens if you want
to be as good as Darren "Cookiehead" Jenkins)—maybe you'll
read this poem. You—an eraserhead with bleached buzz cut,
silver-framed wraparounds & nose/eyebrow/navel rings, who
can grind a 50/50—and I, a middle-aged woman who likes spareribs,
umbrella drinks, Don Ho, & hula—will finally meet. And this
is what I'll say to you: After 47 years I've found a civilized way
to polish my silver. I've created my own tradition with Royal
Copenhagen hand-painted porcelain dinnerware. You should train

to be a children's etiquette consultant at the Protocol School
in Washington, D.C. I'm Marcia from the Psychic Friends Network.
Someday, after you're bald & your wife has dumped you, alone
with refrigerator mold & the cat's litterbox, you'll remember this poem.

THE VIRGIN OF GUADALUPE

Last week, a water stain resembling the face of the Virgin of Guadalupe
was spotted by a janitor on a subway floor-tile. It drew such
a large crowd that the mayor of Mexico City finally had to lift
& install the tile in a shrine above the Hidalgo station, as mariachis
played & worshippers cheered. I'm here in my kitchen grinding lentils
& milk in a blender. When I wash my face with lentils & milk
I feel like Cleopatra. If I add a little seaweed to my bath, light
some candles & play soothing music as I soak, I feel better.
I've just spent a long day writing the *Bully-proofing Your School*
manual for the P.T.A. & I'm tired of explaining how to turn
a taunt into a joke. I'm surrounded by people who
say that if you watch "The Wizard of Oz" with the sound turned
down & play Pink Floyd's "Dark Side of the Moon," using the MGM
lion's third & final roar as the starting point, you'll notice that
the album ends with a fading heartbeat, just as Dorothy
is listening to the tin man's chest. I don't believe in miracles.
If I were sipping Dom Perignon in a restaurant carved into a coastal
hillside, where the air smells of hibiscus & green parrots flutter
in the moonlight, I'd probably start dreaming of Cleveland—
it's not a good cab town & once you get somewhere, it's almost
impossible to get back. I might as well *be* in Cleveland. Where's
the miracle in that? What's the difference between seeing the Virgin
in a water stain & downing shots of pureed wheat grass for your health
or the conjecture that Jayne Mansfield was beheaded in her car accident
outside of New Orleans in June of '67?—the beheading part is hooey.
To be honest, I don't feel like Cleopatra. I feel as if I've been
equipped with waterproof electrodes to monitor my heartbeat.
A 20 lb. weight is strapped to my waist. My feet are tied together.
I'm thrown into the water so that lifeguards can practice rescuing me,
again and again, & I never quite drown. Where's the miracle in that?

A STAR IS BORN IN THE EAGLE NEBULA

—to Larry Levis, 1946-1996

They've finally admitted that trying to save oil-soaked
seabirds is tougher than it looks. You can wash them, rinse them
with a high-pressure nozzle, feed them activated charcoal
to absorb toxic chemicals & test them for anemia, but the oil
still disrupts the microscopic alignment of feathers that creates
a kind of wet suit around the body. We now know that the caramel
coloring in whiskey causes nightmares, & an ingredient in beer
produces hemorrhoids. Glycerol in vodka causes anal seepage,
& when girls enter puberty, the growth of their left ventricles
slows down for about a year. Box office receipts plummeted this week.
Retail sales are sluggish. The price of wheat rose. Soybeans sank.
The Dow is up thirty points. A man named Alan Gerry has bought
Woodstock & plans to build a theme park, a sort of combo
Williamsburg/Disneyland for graying hippies. The weather report
predicts a batch of showers preceding a cold front down
on the Middle Atlantic Coast—you're not missing much.
Day after day at the Ford research labs in Dearborn, Michigan,
an engineer in charge of hood latches labors, measuring the weight
of a hood, calculating the resistance of the latch, coming up
with the perfect closure, the perfect snapping sound,
while the shadow of Jupiter's moon, Io, races across cloud tops
at 10.5 miles a second, and a star is born in the Eagle Nebula.
Molecular hydrogen and dust condenses into lumps that contract
and ignite under their own gravity. In today's paper four girls
in a photo appear to be tied, as if by invisible threads, to five
soap bubbles floating along the street against the black wall
of the Park Avenue underpass. Nothing earthshattering. The girls

are simply *there*. They've blown the bubbles & are following them
up the street. That's the plot. *A life. Any life.* I turn the page,
and Charlie Brown is saying—"Sometimes I lie awake at night
& ask, 'Does anyone remember me?' & a voice comes to me
out of the dark, 'Sure, Frank, we remember you.'"

THE LIGHTER-THAN-AIR SOCIETY

Our missiles have heat-sensing devices. So do snakes. Beetles
that lay their eggs in freshly burned wood can sense forests aflame
30 miles away & are known as Smoke Jumpers. Sixty years ago
today, at 3 p.m., crowds of schoolchildren packed midtown street corners
to see the Hindenburg flying over Manhattan. Three football fields
in length, the Hindenburg, a soaring Queen Mary complete
with aluminum Bluthner grand piano & (according to the Lighter-
Than-Air-Society) doomed because its inside surface of skin
was coated with iron oxide), ignited & burned to the ground in
32 seconds. Why can't the Lighter-Than-Air Society detect the heat
in poems? Poems aren't bloated & don't have huge red,
white & black swastika flags on their tails, but does that mean
they should spontaneously combust on dusty library shelves
all over America? If scientists now believe that life doesn't need
much light to grow—giant clams & fields of tubeworms are perfectly
happy to multiply in volcanic rifts that gird the global seabed
(it turns out that the earth's inner heat releases chemicals
that feed microbes, which in turn start a food chain)—then shouldn't
I be happy growing poetry in the dark? If one stanza is noticed
by one person who is about to waste his time wondering whether
or not the main livingroom area should float on poured concrete pilings
reminiscent of those used as bridge supports, or if he's about to
dedicate his life to testing sounds—windshield wiper swooshes,
hood snaps & the thonk of parking brakes when released—at
the Ford research & development lab in Dearborn, Michigan,
and he comes across, by accident, these lines by Rilke: "Night,
still night, into which are woven/ purely white things. . . brightly
mottled things, scattered colors, which are raised up/ into

One Darkness's One Stillness,—include me"—and he changes his mind,
deciding to go to the Caribbean to study frogs that rain down every
morning from the tops of trees to the forest floors, spreading their legs &
flattening out their bodies like parachutes, falling 100 feet to the ground—
then isn't poetry a flame that ignites the heart even if the members
of the Lighter-Than-Air-Society can't see it? Hello you Smoke Jumpers
out there, who have flown such a long way to alight upon these words.

NOTES

"Augury," lines 28-29: *Metropolitan Home*, September 1996.

"Small Miracles," line 10, "liberating. . .limestone": *Metropolitan Home*, September 1996.

"Twenty Ways to Tie a Sarong," title: *The New York Times,* August 18, 1996. Lines 15-16, and the description of James Levine, *The New York Times,* August 18, 1996.

"Two Fairytale Figures Give Me Advice," quotations in section 1: *Favorite Folktales from Around the World*.

"Fast Lane," line 7: *House Beautiful,* September 1996, p.128. Line 20: *Better Homes & Gardens,* September 1996, p.124. Line 21, "plastic. . . key," and lines 23-26: *Outdoor Life,* August 1996.

"Four Significant Childhoods" pastiches events and quotations from Agatha Christie's *An Autobiography; The Particulars of My Life* by B.F. Skinner; *The Magic Years of Beatrix Potter* by Margaret Lane; and *Lana: The Lady, the Legend, the Truth*: by Lana Turner.

"Menagerie of Strangers," line 1, "Isle of Youth's. . .relax us": *Islands,* June 1997. Line 10: *Elle,* July 1997, p. 58. Section 2, idea for golf ball diving: *Hemispheres,* October 1996, p.45. Section 3, line 14, "One Egg Diorama. . . sand": *Michael's Arts & Crafts Magazine,* December 1996. The image of the bear curling back its rubbery lips, and the title of Section 3: *Outdoor Life*, August 1996. Golf terminology is borrowed from an article on Laura Davies in *Hemispheres,* September 1996. Section 4, line 6, "cut chines. . . rasp": *Wooden Boat Magazine,* October 1997. Line 10, "You scuttled. . . north": *Field & Stream*, October 1996.

"The Winter of Our Discontent," line 5, "It's time. . .steering"; and line 7, "yellow. . . antler": *Outdoor Life,* August 1996.

"Poets Anonymous," line 10: *Country Living,* December 1996, p. 80. Lines 15-17: *Better Homes & Gardens,* September 1996, p. 124. Line 18, "We've zigzagged. . .Mexico": *Travel & Leisure*, September 1996.

"Earthly Light," line 13, "laceleaf. . .waterfall": *Better Homes & Gardens*, September 1996, p.108. The description of restoring heaven is adapted from a description of restoring Buckingham Palace that appeared in *The New York Times*.

"Black Pearls," line 24, "Beneath. . . day": *National Geographic,* June 1997, p. 21. Line 29: *The New York Times Magazine*, July 27, 1997, p. 27.

"A Portrait of Larry with Trogons": A trogon is a brightly colored tropical bird.

"Psychic Friends Network," lines 25-29, pastiches quotes borrowed from *Martha Stewart Living,* November 1996.

"A Star is Born in the Eagle Nebula": The description of four girls & soap bubbles is based on Sarah Boxer's discussion of a photograph by Helen Levitt in *The New York Times,* May 9, 1997.

ACKNOWLEDGMENTS

The American Poetry Review: "The Winter of Our Discontent and Other Seasons," "A Portrait of Larry with Trogons," and "Augury."

Colorado Review: "Fast Lane."

Connecticut Review: "Kriya."

Crazy Horse: "A Vacation in Boca Isn't Rilke," "A Saturday Night at the Flying Dog," "The World's Greatest Electrician," and "Psychic Friends Network."

Denver Quarterly: "Earthly Light."

Field: "The Amish on Rollerblades," "Black Pearls," and "The Tunnel of Love."

The Gettysburg Review: "A Star is Born in the Eagle Nebula."

Harvard Review: "Medusa, 1996."

Kenyon Review: "Notes from the Tower."

North American Review: "The Magic Broom."

Prairie Schooner: "Agatha Christie," "Beatrix Potter," "Depression," "Fear," "Sloth & Torpor," "Anxiety," "Ecstasy," "Stone Worship," "Small Miracles," "My Sisters, the Oysters," and "Why I Hang Out With Nerds."

Southern Review: "Lana Turner."

Virginia Quarterly Review: "B.F. Skinner."

"Earthly Light" was reprinted in *The Pushcart Prize Anthology*.

"A Saturday Night at the Flying Dog" and "A Portrait of Larry with Trogons" were reprinted in *Contemporary American Poetry: A Bread Loaf Anthology*.

Thanks to David St. John, Charles Wright, Thomas Lux, Charles Simic, and Nick Levis for their comments and encouragement. And thanks to Stanley Plumly, whose suggestions reshaped this book entirely, giving it a better sense of continuity. Without Murray Gell-Mann, who corrected many logical flaws in early drafts and edited many revisions, this book could not have been completed.

ABOUT THE AUTHOR

Marcia Southwick grew up on the East Coast and currently lives in Santa Fe with her husband, the physicist Murray Gell-Mann. She is the author of two previously published volumes of poetry, and her work has been included in numerous anthologies.

COLOPHON

Designed by Steve Farkas. Composed by Professional Book Compositors using Clearface 11 point text type and 14 point Washout display type. Printed and perfect bound by Cushing-Malloy using 60# Glatfelter offset acid-free paper.